My FATHER'S Hands

My FATHER'S Hands

52 reasons to trust *God* with your heart

Christy Fitzwater

© 2016 by Christy Fitzwater

Published by christyfitzwater.com

Printed in the United States of America

Cover design by Chautona Havig
Cover photos mycola/thinkstock.com, KonstantinChristian/ shutterstock
Cover fonts Adorn Garland Regular, Jailbird Jenna Regular, Baskerville Old Face Regular

ISBN 978-1981436972

Introduction

The first time we had lunch was at Bonelli's Bistro. While I ate my panini with slabs of mozzarella cheese oozing out the sides, we found we had something in common: both of our dads served in Vietnam. My dad came home. She lost hers when she was only two years old.

She told me about her new stepdad and the years of sexual abuse she suffered at his hands. Her heart longed to know God, but there was so much pain in the way. A lot of tears fell over our Italian food that day.

Because I am a pastor's wife, people tell me their personal stories. I know some people had dads who were there but were not really present. Some had dads who favored one child over the other. Some people were raised by a single mom, and they never knew their father. I have heard stories of people whose dads were alcoholics or were abusive or both. Some had fathers who were neglectful or simply cool and distant.

One young adult sent me this note:

I wish I could know what a loving parent is like. I've grown up without any idea how a loving parent acts. My parents were both deeply broken and insecure people who had no idea how to love or be loved. When I came over to cook dinner for you all, I was amazed at how much you guys actually like each other and enjoy being together, and would choose that over almost anything. I asked myself, "That's how a real family works?"

I have never seen that or experienced it. I was trying to get away from my family as early as age 6, because I've never known what it's like to be wanted by others, made a priority, sought after at a heart level, and beyond any danger of "blowing it." I have no concept of a God whose intentions are in my favor. Just a God who stands by and lets me get hurt over and over.

I know God is trying to heal that part of me, but it's like asking me to grow a new heart and completely rebuild my mind. I'm so conditioned to thinking of myself as pathetic and alone that I don't know any other way to live. It's going to take a lot of time and a lot of love from God in order to change this, and I just don't have any idea where to go from here.

Without meaning to, we approach God expecting Him to be just like our dads on earth. But there are so many different kinds of dads, so many flavors. How do we know which characteristics are true of God? Is He the deserter? The abuser? The negligent? The critical? The doting? Who is He? And can we trust Him enough to put our fragile hearts in His hands?

More than anything, I want you to know about entitlement – not the disgusting entitlement that comes to mind when we think of rotten, demanding children, but the kind of entitlement that lifts the chin of a child and gives him a sense of value and permission to live.

In Malcolm Gladwell's book, *Outliers: The Story of Success*, he contrasts the parenting differences between the upper/middle classes and the lower class. In wealthier families, parents tend to teach their children a healthy entitlement. Kids are encouraged to speak up for themselves. They learn they are valuable and that it is okay for them to reason and negotiate with those who are in authority. Gladwell contrasts this with parenting in poor families, where children often learn to distrust authority and to constrain themselves around authority, becoming unhealthily independent. Gladwell says, "Constraint may seem like a small thing" but it can be "a crippling handicap in navigating the world." As I read about these parenting styles, I realized that the way we've been parented has a profound effect on how we approach God as Father. I believe that from a dad, a person might learn a constraint that later cripples his relationship with God.

My dad grew up in poverty, but he worked hard in the oil fields, saved and invested wisely, and eventually came very close to being a millionaire. He was rich. You will see, as you read vignettes about my experiences with Dad, that he entitled me to come to him, to ask for help whenever I needed it. He showed himself to be trustworthy, and I knew I could depend on him. So I came to God with entitlement embedded in my heart, and I found God to be the same kind of Father as my dad.

God is rich and powerful. He tells us over and over to come to Him, to ask for help and provision. He repeatedly says in the Bible that He is faithful, and we can trust Him. God also gives us value, seen in the loving sacrifice He made for us in the death of His Son. God even encourages us to negotiate with Him in prayer. He clearly rewards those who hound Him incessantly until they get what they need. It's an astounding relationship if we come into it understanding what it means to be an entitled child.

Let me prove this whole entitlement idea to you with one verse from the book of Hebrews. The author spends a lot of time telling us how awesome Jesus is, and how Jesus has made a way for us to come to the Father. Then he gives this instruction: "Let us then with confidence draw near to the throne of grace, that we may receive mercy and find grace to help in time of need" (Hebrews 4:16). Do you hear it? Permission to approach: that's what rich kids experience. They just march up to their dad, with no fear, and ask for whatever they need. God, from a throne where He exhibits His great wealth and power, lifts the chin of His child and says, "Tell me what you need."

Gladwell says that people raised in poverty tend to cower and avert their eyes when facing authority, but the writer of Hebrews tells us to approach God with confidence. We're entitled to come to the Father with backs straight and to look Him directly in the eyes. We make our requests with complete expectation that we're going to walk away with what we've asked. We know His hands are open and welcoming to us. It seems too good to be true, but this is real. This is what it means to be a part of the kingdom of God.

One time my cousin's wife, only half-jokingly, said to me, "You're spoiled by your dad. But at least you know it. I guess that makes it okay." Yes, I have been spoiled by my dad, and I know it. The bad part about that is not being able to share that spoiled life with you. My dad only had enough energy and resources to spoil my brother and me. He entitled only two kids. But God also spoils me by His entitlement, and how well I know that. The good news is that I can share this with you. You, too, can be adopted by God and know what it's like to be raised in the upper class of God's Kingdom.

I am writing this book for those of you who did not know your dad, or who had the kind of dad who caused you pain, inside or out. Maybe when you see the word "Father" in the Bible, it makes you draw back. You want to know God, but you can't get past that word. Along the way you have learned *not* to trust authority and instead to make your own way in the world. I hope my stories will help you unlearn that way of thinking when it comes to knowing God as Father.

I am letting you borrow a look at my dad, a not-so-perfect man, who managed to show me that I was deeply loved, and I could trust him. Because of how my dad cared for me, I can come to God as a Father and expect good from Him. I hope the following stories will give you the courage to put your life into God's care and allow Him to be everything a perfect Father should be.

Now Jesus was praying in a certain place, and when he finished, one of his disciples said to him, "Lord, teach us to pray, as John taught his disciples." And he said to them, "When you pray, say: 'Father...'"

~ Luke 11:1-2

"The best fathers hold fledgling hearts in calloused hands without bruising them."

~ Sara Hagerty

Contents

1

SOMEONE TO

Rejoice

OVER YOU

From a deep sleep, I would feel it, something warm and scratchy in my ear. It was the lightest touch, just enough to tickle. I would endure it for a few seconds, and then I would reach up to brush it away. It was the calloused hand of my dad, with his finger in my ear serving as an odd but affectionate alarm clock. Then came the singing:

Good morning, little sunshine,
How did you wake so soon?
The sun is in the sky,
And you scared away the moon.

It was mostly awful – on purpose – and led me to

19

groan, "Daaaaaaaaad." (If you extend the vowels long enough and accentuate them properly, you can also communicate: *Leave me alone and let me sleep longer.*)

My family? We sing to each other. Only a few have the kind of voice you would put in front of a microphone, but we sing anyway. Singing comes from a cheerful, affectionate heart, and the silly songs become worn and comfortable, like your favorite pair of slippers.

The prophet Zephaniah says to God's people: "The LORD your God is in your midst, a mighty one who will save; he will rejoice over you with gladness; he will quiet you by his love; he will exult over you with loud singing" (Zephaniah 3:17). God is mighty, but He loves you and wants to sing loudly and cheerfully over your life.

> WRITE YOUR RESPONSE TO THIS IMAGE
> OF GOD SINGING OVER YOU.

2

SOMEONE TO

Meet

YOUR BASIC NEEDS

There was one source of heat in our home, a black Benjamin Franklin stove that sat on top of a square of brick flooring in the living room. Somewhere between the time Mom stopped catting around and went to bed and the time my early-bird father woke up, that fire would usually go out completely.

In Wyoming, it was not unusual for the winter temperature to hover around zero degrees for weeks. Sometimes a little above zero. Sometimes a lot below.

The first out of bed, Dad would empty an armful of wood into that Benjamin Franklin, which was engineered in a perfect criss-cross for maximum air movement. He would add a slug of solvent as a starter, the safety of which will not be discussed in this book. Then he would light a match and throw it in.

Whoooooof. A fire would roar to life. (Excuse me, but I had to go ask my husband what sound effect solvent makes when a flame hits it. For your reading instruction, he insists this *whoof* has to start in the chest and not from the throat. He made me practice.)

If perhaps there were still coals left from the night before, Dad would stack the wood on top of the coals and then pull the wooden bellows down from its hook on the brick wall behind the fireplace. Gently, Dad would pump the bellows to blow air on those hot coals, and coax them to light his fire. I loved the bellows and the magic of the flames.

It was such a lovely fire, but the heat was reluctant to travel to the rest of the house very quickly in the morning. Before getting dressed, I would take my clothes out to the fireplace and heat first my backside, to the point of first-degree burns, and then turn around and hold my cold jeans and shirt in front of the fire. I rotated through this routine like a marshmallow on a stick.

My dad cut down trees, loaded them into a truck, unloaded them from the truck, hand chopped them into firewood pieces, stacked them in the back yard, went out in the snow every day regardless of the weather, brought in wood, and built a fire. He kept that fire going every day, all winter long.

I feel sorry for the girls who grew up with gas or electric heat. There is no heroism in turning up a thermostat. I was warm in February in Wyoming, at six o'clock in the morning, which is the Western equivalent of walking over a gentleman's coat laid across a puddle.

In the Psalms, we read: "For he is our God, and we are the people of his pasture, and the sheep of his hand" (Psalm 95:7). I think if the psalmist had been from Wyoming, he would have sung, "He is our God, and we are the people for whom his hands cut firewood and pump bellows." There is a rustic chivalry to having someone strong taking care of your daily needs. God will take care of you in this way, without fail.

WHAT IS AN EXAMPLE OF A BASIC NEED

GOD HAS CARED FOR IN YOUR LIFE?

Journaling

3

Someone to

Be

with You

The movie was *Escape to Witch Mountain* and I brought home a picture so I could enter the coloring contest hosted by the theater. (I have never again seen a coloring contest hosted by a theater).

How it went from being me with the coloring page to me and Dad at the front room table working on it together, I do not know. Did I ask him to help me? Or did he happen by and insist?

So there we were at the table: me with colored pencils and an eraser, Dad with his coloring game face on. Dad taught me how to "color" (I believe Dad's definition of this activity and mine were different) with a certain pressure to create a darker color or with a lighter pressure of the hand to create a lighter color. I called my mother and asked how old I was when I entered this coloring contest. She says I was about seven years old. Of course, you know this is the natural time in a child's life when she becomes keenly aware of the subtle shading required when doing adequate work for a coloring contest.

Let's talk about the eraser. I cannot imagine that the eraser was my idea, and now that I am a parent I wonder that an eraser became part of the equipment necessary for a child to enter a coloring contest. And if you were wondering what the eraser was for, it was to remove the half-millimeter markings I might have colored outside of the lines.

Before you judge my dad, you must know that he was an incredibly patient, albeit intense teacher. He explained things very well. He gave you his full attention. He made you work until something was done to perfection. This coloring page is a sweet memory for me. (However, my husband is a licensed professional counselor, and I think I may ask him later if he thinks perhaps I am repressing anything.)

So I colored this picture. I use the word "I" loosely. I wrote my name on it and turned it in. I won the coloring contest. Your sense of justice might be rising within you at this time. You may think I had an unfair advantage over the other children, but may I request that you only look at my side of things for now?

My dad spent an entire evening with me. I would say that it was good for me to be near my dad while we worked on my picture – receiving his undivided attention. I was being given the unfair advantage of time, and it was wonderful.

The psalmist sings, "For me it is good to be near God" (Psalm 73:28a). God is a Father who wants to be near you, helping you with the details of your life. He will give you His full attention, for as long as you're willing to sit and receive it. It's really good to be near the Father.

YOU HAVE GOD'S ATTENTION.

WHAT WOULD YOU LIKE TO SAY TO HIM?

4

SOMEONE WHO
Wants
YOU TO EXIST

He was in Vietnam when I was born. It was six weeks before he would be stateside and see me for the first time.

There is a letter in my baby book, in his handwriting. (If you are young, let me explain that in 1969 there was a product called "paper," and those who wished to communicate would write on the paper and pay someone to deliver it to the party to whom they wished to speak.) On the top of this letter my dad wrote, in large block letters, "WHOOPY DING!"

And so I know he was glad that I was born.

Now that I have children of my own, I realize how precious that day of birth is. On every birthday of our children, my husband and I reminisce about the trip to the hospital, the labor and delivery, and how we felt when that new little one was put into our arms for the first time. The joy we felt was indescribable.

In Ephesians 1:4-5, Paul says that God "chose us in him before the foundation of the world, that we should be holy and blameless before him. In love he predestined us for adoption as sons through Jesus Christ, according to the purpose of his will." Before you were born, God wanted you. He made plans to adopt you. He chose you.

> KNOWING THAT GOD SHOUTS,
> "WHOOPY DING!" OVER YOUR BIRTH INTO
> HIS FAMILY, HOW DOES THAT GIVE
> YOUR LIFE MEANING NOW?

Journaling

5

L et's play a little word association game. What do you think of when you hear the following titles?

Bridge over the River Kwai

The Longest Day

The Guns of Navarone

Tora! Tora! Tora!

The Great Escape

The Dirty Dozen

Sands of Iwo Jima

Midway

The Green Berets

First Blood

Do you know what this list means to me? My childhood movies. I can hear the men in the prison camp whistling. I can picture the look on the faces of the Japanese when they realized they were not going to win the battle of Midway. I can picture Sylvester Stallone sewing shut the wound in his arm while hiding in a tree. I can still feel the camaraderie of the Dirty Dozen, who turned out to make a pretty good name for themselves after all.

Dad made me watch just about every documentary and movie made on war. While you were listening to Dick Van Dyke sing "Chitty Chitty Bang Bang," I was seeing the emaciated bodies of Jews through the barbed fence of Auschwitz. I was looking at Vietnam POWs hanging from trees with blood dripping. Picture me as a child – with a horrified expression. Dad would lean forward in his chair and say to me, with great sobriety, "You need to see this. These things will happen again, and you need to be prepared." After we watched a World War II prison camp movie, he would ask, "What would you do if you were in that place?"

I recently brought home a keepsake box of mine, filled with all things important from my childhood. In this box was a comic book depiction of *The Hiding Place*, the story of Corrie ten Boom's experience in a World War II death camp. This summarizes my childhood.

You need to know that God is not the kind of Father who says life is going to be rosy. That would be a cruel untruth. Jesus tells His disciples, "I have said these things to you, that in me you may have peace. In the world you will have tribulation. But take heart; I have overcome the world" (John 16:33). God cares enough to look you in the eyes and say that life is going to be hard, and He works to prepare you for what is coming. In the middle of all that scary talk, He wants you to feel peaceful because you aren't taking on the world alone. He can navigate through history, and He has taken care of everything.

> WHAT WORLD EVENTS ARE SCARING YOU TO DEATH?
> HOW DOES KNOWING GOD AS YOUR FATHER GIVE
> YOU PEACE IN THE MIDDLE OF ALL THIS?

Journaling

6

Someone to

Be Gentle

WITH YOU

He came home from the oil field and told me to follow him into the backyard. In his hands was his long metal lunch box, with a black plastic handle. In the backyard, we knelt down on the grass, while Dad slowly opened the lunch box and pulled out a bunny. He let me hold the bunny and pet it. The next day he took it back to the oil field and let it go free.

I was recently talking to an older man who is an army vet and who rides a Harley Davidson. He surprised me when he told me about finding a bunny whose momma he had inadvertently killed with a lawn mower. He said he and his wife took the bunny to the vet and then brought it home and fed it with an eyedropper, through many sleepless nights. This story reminds me of my dad who was a navy vet and an oil field hand, but who was so tender with a bunny.

In Genesis 1:25, we read: "And God made the beasts of the earth according to their kinds and the livestock according to their kinds, and everything that creeps on the ground according to its kind. And God saw that it was good." God created rabbits and thought they were good. He is a mighty warrior, but imagine Him treating you as gently as He would a bunny.

In what ways do you feel

small and fragile today?

Write to God about how you feel

and what you need.

7

Someone to Give You

Over-the-Top

HELP

It was sixth grade and time for the bug-collecting science project. (Why? Why do teachers do these things?) So I bravely collected grasshoppers and butterflies and other such creepy crawlies. I asked Dad to help me make a display for them.

Dad got some wood and fashioned a box. Then he made a lid with a glass inlay. He stained the box and the lid, and he used hinges to attach the lid to the box. He secured a metal hook as a closing mechanism. Then he covered a square of Styrofoam with velvet and placed it inside the box.I put the bugs onto the velvet with pins, because this was my project.

My bug display was of a different class than the bug

collections of the other sixth graders. Pity them.

It was a ridiculously unfair amount of help I got from Dad on that project, but that was a normal part of my experience as his daughter. This is what it's like to have God as a Father, too.

Paul tells the Ephesian believers, "Now to him who is able to do far more abundantly than all we ask or think, according to the power at work within us, to him be glory in the church and in Christ Jesus throughout all generations, forever and ever. Amen." (Ephesians 3:20-21)

God helps His people, but it's never a fair amount of help. I find when I pray to the Lord, He always goes a little overboard. It's always an *abundant* help – never plain Styrofoam. More like a hand-crafted, glass-encased kind of help that raises eyebrows.

> WHAT DO YOU NEED HELP WITH RIGHT NOW?
>
> WRITE A STATEMENT OF BELIEF BELOW,
>
> ADMITTING GOD CAN DO MORE THAN YOU ASK
>
> OR EVEN IMAGINE IN THIS CIRCUMSTANCE.

Journaling

8

SOMEONE TO

Stand

IN HARM'S WAY FOR YOU

When I was young, Dad hunted foxes and coyotes. Among the tools in the garage hung wooden racks strung with furs, which Dad would sell for profit. I'm sure he did this partly out of a love for hunting, but also out of his work ethic. He saw a way to make money using only some elbow grease, so he took advantage of it.

One night he tried to get a shot off at a fox. He missed. As he lowered the gun onto his lap, he unconsciously held his left hand over the barrel. Here I must tell you that Dad was not foolish with guns. This was a rare moment of thoughtlessness for him. Something on the seat caught the trigger, and the gun fired. The truck window was rolled down, and he heard the glass break inside the door.

Then he noticed a tuft of fabric coming out of his glove.

Arriving at the hospital, he was told his left index finger could be saved, but it would always be fixed in a certain position. He did not like that idea, so he opted for them to remove the finger.

I remember sitting in the waiting room at the hospital.

I remember when he came home with a huge white bandage around his hand, and we had to be careful around him.

I remember how sad he was the day he finally was able to grab a stack of Oreos with his left hand, but the Oreos fell to the floor. That was the only time I saw him upset about the loss of his finger.

Dad squeezed a rubber ball to regain strength in his hand. He had one more surgery to deal with a nerve issue. Then he cut all the index fingers off his left-hand gloves and kept on living.

The missing finger became a game, to amuse children and unsuspecting adults. Dad would hold up his hand quickly and do a little math game. Math is not my thing, so I will not even try to explain this to you. All I know is that everyone eventually said "Ten!" and Dad would laugh.

Jesus did His own hand trick with Thomas when He said, "Put your finger here, and see my hands; and put out your hand, and place it in my side. Do not disbelieve, but believe." (John 20:27) God has something to show you in the hands of His Son. Jesus was wounded, but not out of carelessness with a firearm. His hands took the wounds, the punishment for your sin, so that you could be in relationship with the Father. Jesus holds out His wounded hands, so you can see how much the Father loves you. He loves you so much.

WRITE A THANK YOU TO THE FATHER,

FOR THIS LOVE SHOWN TO YOU

IN THE WOUNDED HANDS OF JESUS.

Journaling

9

D ad attached an old-fashioned hand-crank wringer to the front of the house. This was for the chamois, because every day or so, Dad would wash our vehicles.

I say "wash," but I mean the kind of wash that causes other people to stop in front of the house and ask, "Could I pay you to detail my car?"

I mean wash with soap and suds and then open the doors and clean the inside edge where your dirty feet leave marks.

I mean scrub the windshield with ammonia until all the bug guts are removed.

Then came the chamois, and not a drop of water was left on the car. This was followed by tire spray, so the shiny black sidewalls would impress the neighbors.

One time I "washed" my car at Dad's house, and he was disgusted.

"Is this how you wash your dishes at home?" he said. "If so, I'm never eatin' at your house."

So I guess I may have missed some spots.

Paul talks about "our great God and Savior Jesus Christ who gave himself for us to redeem us from all lawlessness and to purify for himself a people for his own possession who are zealous for good works" (Titus 2:13-14). Just like my dad and his cars, God likes His possessions to be spotless. The Father made a great investment to purify you, in a way that will make people ask, "Hey, can God do that for me?"

Think about all the details my dad put into a car.
Now consider the dirty places in your soul.
List a few parts of your inner person
that you long for God to clean.

Journaling

10

Someone You Can

Follow

INTO SCARY PLACES

Once a week Dad would splurge, and we would go out to eat in downtown Lander. (It was a full three-minute drive from our house, on one end of town, to Dairy Land on the other end.) Dairy Land is the home of the cheese wheel, which is a hamburger patty and cheese dipped in batter and fried. I'm not sure where this falls on the food pyramid.

Dad would always order a butterscotch malt, with extra malt. Then we would sit as a family and laugh and enjoy the luxury of burgers and fries.

Dad would have me hold out my hand flat on the table. Then he would make a fist and bring it down hard on my hand. "See? It doesn't hurt to do that." It was like some kind of Wyoming family carnival trick. Every week. (This was before cable was in full swing, I imagine.)

"Hold out your hand."

"Dad, no."

"It won't hurt," he would say. He would gently stretch my hand out flat on the table. Then he would smash it.

It was kind of cool, really, because it didn't hurt. But I was always hesitant. And he would always assure me it wouldn't hurt. He wanted me to trust him.

On more than one occasion, God has asked me to do something that I thought would hurt, like the time he asked me to go teach a Bible study in Uganda. Every night for months leading up to it, I cried with fear about that trip.

"It's scary," I told the Lord.

"You'll be okay," He said to me.

And I was.

In Psalm 56:3, we read, "When I am afraid, I put my trust in you" (Psalm 56:3). You can lay out your life in front of God and trust Him. You *can* trust Him. It's scary, but cool.

Describe a time when you trusted God,
even though you were afraid to do
what He was asking you to do.

Journaling

11

SOMEONE TO

Correct

YOU

One summer day, I sat in the living room next to Dad. My little brother, Arie, had just received flippers for his birthday, and I listened to Dad make plans to take him to the swimming pool to try them out.

"I want to go!" I said.

Dad refused my request. "No, not this time," he said.

I was crushed, and then begged and begged to go with them.

"Your brother wants to do things with you all the time, and you won't let him. It's his turn to do something fun. No, you may not go," he said.

So I did not go. I stayed home and thought about how I had treated my brother.

I've experienced this same kind of discipline from the Lord, most often in my roles as wife and mom. I don't know how many times God's Spirit has bluntly said to me, "Hey, that was a little harsh with your kid, don't ya think?" or "Should you act that arrogant towards your man?" This kind of confrontation is zero fun, but it has made me a better woman.

The psalmist sings, "Blessed is the man whom you discipline, O LORD, and whom you teach out of your law" (Psalm 94:12). It is a blessing to have a Father who cares enough to discipline you. God is not a Father who always says "Yes" so that you'll be happy in the moment. He wants to develop character in you, so that you can experience all kinds of happiness down the road because of who you have become.

WHAT IS ONE WAY GOD HAS DISCIPLINED YOU, IN ORDER TO DEVELOP CHARACTER IN YOU?

Journaling

12

We were in Dad's little aluminum boat one summer day, in the middle of Shoshoni Lake. The boys had fishing poles in their hands and we girls had books, when without warning, a furious storm came up. In the Rocky Mountains, at an elevation of almost 8,000 feet, the weather can go from delightful to scary in just a few minutes.

Dad got us to the nearest shore, which was opposite from our campsite, and we huddled under trees until the brief summer storm passed. We were all soaked and dangerously cold by the time it was over. Then Dad got us in the boat and went as quickly to our campsite as his old boat motor would go.

I'll never forget how Dad went to battle to get us all

dry and warm. Within minutes, my violently shivering body was in dry clothes and tucked under layers of heavy sleeping bags and flannel quilts. Dad knelt at the end of my air mattress and reached for my feet underneath the quilts. His calloused hands rubbed my feet until they were warm and my body had stopped shaking.

I don't remember him taking care of his own wet clothes.

Several years ago, I went through another storm, when my husband had a severe reaction to medication that left him chronically ill for a few years. Through the whole experience, I was keenly aware of God taking care of me in a very personal way. One night, when I felt the most alone, when I felt unable to endure the difficulty of what I was going through, I called out to the Lord. As I lay down in bed, I picked up a devotional book to read, and I remember the devotion spoke exactly to what I had just prayed to the Lord. It felt like that night when my dad rubbed my feet until they got warm. It was one of the most special times I have ever had with the Lord.

Daniel 6:27a says, "He delivers and rescues." You are coming to a Father who will be with you through the storms. He is going to make sure you're okay, from start to finish.

So what storm are you going through right now? Write out a call to help, and tell God what you need from Him right now.

Journaling

13

SOMEONE TO
Go Ahead
OF YOU

Those summers at Shoshoni Lake were wonderful. Dad would make a trip the day before to set up camp. Then he would come back for the book readers. We would pile into the four-wheel drive Bronco and make the three-hour, bone-jarring ride into the lake. Though only a few miles long, the "road" was actually a boulder-strewn dry creek bed. Sometimes we girls would get out and walk a bit while Dad maneuvered the Bronco between boulders.

This seemed like normal summer activity to me.

We would drive up and up. Then there would be a place where we would break out of the trees and could look down on the lake. It was beautiful and solitary, just the way my Dad liked it. Curse the man who might suggest improving the road to the lake so that more people could have access.

Going down close to the "beach" (we make do in Wyoming), we would come to the 12-man canvas tent Dad had set up the day before. This is where the real camping would begin, and I would pull out my book and get all cozy in a sleeping bag to read for the afternoon.

Dad took care of everything. He cooked all the meals and took us out in the boat. Mom was an indoor girl like me, and he made sure it was a very pleasant experience for her to come camping.

Then we would go home a few days later, dusty and battered from the drive, to watch Dad fillet the biggest lake trout, exposing their pink insides. Meanwhile, Mom would make the beer batter.

Gasp. My little Southern Baptist heart had to stretch uncomfortably in order to eat fish dipped in beer batter without imagining I was going straight to hell for consuming alcohol, even though Mom assured me the alcohol cooked out. But those fish were so good.

Camping with Dad: it wasn't Disneyland, but in those days, I didn't know I needed anything more than a family, a canvas tent, and beer-battered trout to be happy.

One of the great benefits of having God as a Father is

that He is able to anticipate what we are going to need, and He can go ahead to prepare things for our future. The psalmist sings, "The LORD is my shepherd; I shall not want" (Psalm 23:1). Shepherds go ahead of the sheep and make sure their needs are cared for. You are coming to a Father who will take care of all the details in advance.

WHAT DOES YOUR CALENDAR

LOOK LIKE THIS WEEK?

ASK GOD TO GO AHEAD OF YOU

AND PREPARE WHAT YOU NEED

FOR ALL OF YOUR ACTIVITIES.

Journaling

14

> SOMEONE TO BE
> *Well-Intentioned*
> TOWARD YOU

When I was little, in the summer we would go to my grandparent's cabin outside of Dubois, Wyoming. This was a fun place, with turquoise metal cabinets from the fifties, an outdoor pump that ran water so cold it could give you hypothermia if you didn't wash your hair fast enough, and an outhouse in the backyard. The backyard was landscaped in sagebrush, just like the front. There was a loft in the cabin, with two queen beds and two twin beds that looked out between the slats of the railing. From the loft, we children would tie a string to a bucket and raise and lower things to each other all day long.

There was also a creek along the dirt road in front of the cabin, and we would walk down there and throw some rocks into the water.

One summer, Dad took his motorcycle with us to Dubois. Mom had a motorcycle, too. Now that I am a wife of 23 years, I consider that this makes her a mighty fine woman, seeing as how she preferred book reading and cross-stitching and all.

We hopped on the motorcycles one afternoon, me sitting in front of Dad. It was just a slow, casual ride up a dirt trail, but something happened along the trail. My head went forward, and my teeth met up with the handlebar. (I cringed even as I wrote that.)

I was very young when this happened, but I clearly remember Dad scurrying down a steep embankment, to wet a piece of cloth in the ice-cold water of the creek down below. He gently pulled my front teeth back into place and cleaned up the blood.

This damage turned my front teeth permanently yellow, and Dad blamed himself for that. My yellow teeth only come to my mind when a preschooler with no filter says, "Why are your front teeth yellow?" They may be yellow, but I never lost those teeth because of Dad's quick action.

In remembering this story, I see my dad's fallibility. He was unable to foresee the injury and, in the moment, was unable to stop it. But what rises to the top, in my mind, is that he wanted good for me. This is the man who later forked out thousands for me to have braces. He cared about my teeth and my smile.

God is not fallible. He doesn't experience "accidents" that take him by surprise. But he does allow hard things to happen in our lives. In the middle of these hard times, however, he is a Father who is well-intentioned toward us. Psalm 40:11 says, "As for you, O LORD, you will not restrain your mercy from me; your steadfast love and your faithfulness will ever preserve me!" God is a Father who cares about you. Your life may not be perfect, the way you would choose it to be, but the Father will preserve you.

> HOW HAVE GOD'S LOVE AND FAITHFULNESS
> BEEN EVIDENT TO YOU THROUGH
> PAINFUL OR DAMAGING CIRCUMSTANCES?
> HOW HAVE YOU EXPERIENCED
> HIS GOOD INTENTIONS TOWARD YOU?

Journaling

15

SOMEONE TO GIVE YOU A

Song

Dad considered Wyoming to be the perfect place, and if other people would please stay out, that would be fine with him. So most of our recreation happened in Wyoming, but sometimes we had other adventures.

One time my mom and Dad and I, along with my aunt and uncle and my cousin, loaded up in a sedan and drove to Mount Rushmore. We had an eight-track player and only one eight-track tape. This lone tape was by the Sons of the Pioneers, one of Dad's favorite singing groups. Because of this, I never want to hear the song "Cool Water," ever again.

Dad loved music and played the guitar (before he shot off his finger.) He loved any group that had a good bass singer and tight harmony. Of course, his own mother played accordion and tap danced in the kitchen, so we had to have music in our family.

Recently we took our baby to college, and you know that's hard on a momma's heart. On our way to Texas, we stopped at my mom's and went with her to the little church where I grew up. On that Sunday, a man sang a song that he had written. The chorus repeated this line: "Nothing stays the same except Jesus." I hummed that chorus all the way to Texas and back.

It was just like God to stick a tune in my mind: something encouraging to sing through the pain of letting go of my son.

Psalm 33:2 says, "Give thanks to the LORD with the lyre; make melody to him with the harp of ten strings!" There is an emotional warmth to a person who is stirred by melody, who will cry over a sad song and who can't help but move his feet to a driving rhythm. And this Father who loves you is a God of music. He can understand your heart's greatest joy and feel the pain of your deepest grief. Very often He will put a song in your heart, to encourage and comfort you.

HOW HAVE YOU SEEN GOD
USE MUSIC IN HIS RELATIONSHIP
WITH YOU?

Journaling

16

SOMEONE TO

Hold

YOUR SHAKING HANDS

In sixth grade, I started playing the piano for church because they were desperate.

I received conflicting messages about the tempo of the songs. The pastor's wife, who led the hymn singing, apparently wanted to be able to breathe between verses. Dad, however, wanted a toe-tapping speed. I'm not sure either one of them was ever completely satisfied.

I was nervous before I would go up to play the piano, so Dad would grab my cold, damp hands and sandwich them between his. He would rub until my hands were warm, and until his encouragement sank in. This also served as exfoliation, as the skin of his blue-collar hands had long ago been replaced by calluses.

Every Sunday I played a "special," while the deacons in their good Sunday jeans took up the offering. In Southern Baptist terms, a special was some entertainment while the offering plate was being passed. It was a Wyoming version of Carnegie Hall, as far as Dad was concerned: a reason to be proud of his girl.

"Ya done good," he would whisper (not very discreetly) in my ear when I sat down. Then he would pat my back so hard it hurt.

I'm sure you know how it feels to face something that makes your palms sweaty, and for you I offer Psalm 139:5: "You hem me in, behind and before, and lay your hand upon me." God will come before you, to warm your shaking hands, as you go out to do the scary and uncomfortable tasks of life. He will come behind you, to pat you on the back and celebrate what you have done.

DESCRIBE A TIME WHEN GOD
GAVE YOU COURAGE WHEN
YOU WERE NERVOUS ABOUT SOMETHING.

Journaling

17

SOMEONE TO

Believe

IN YOUR GIFTS

For eight dollars a week, and for eleven years, Dad paid for me to go across the street to take piano lessons from Mrs. Meredith, and then later to attend college piano lessons.

I practiced the piano for hours every night.

Well, I played the piano for hours every night. I think we all know the difference there.

Dad had significant hearing loss from working radar in airplanes over Vietnam, so the TV was always loud. "Dad, could you pleeeease turn down the television?" I would holler from my place on the piano stool in the front room. He would turn it down a bit. A very little bit.

"Soft pedal it!" he would holler not too much later. (Although I think it is unfair that the man who prodded me to play louder and with more energy at church suddenly wanted me to play soft-like. Parents are confusing sometimes.)So I would soft pedal it a bit. A very little bit.

But he never asked me to stop. Not one time. He never came out to the front room and politely let me know my piano pounding was driving him crazy as he was trying to relax in the evening.

So I just kept playing.

In Psalm 33:3, we are instructed to, "Sing to him a new song; play skillfully on the strings, with loud shouts." I love the word "skillfully" in that verse. God appreciates when we do things skillfully in His honor. I once talked to a friend who told me her parents never went to anything she did. She never saw her dad cheering her on at the activities in which she was involved. She never had parents telling her "Good job!" after a game. But be assured that God listens and watches when you use your special skills. God will invest in you. He has given you unique gifts and talents, and he wants you to use them.

> SO WHAT CAN YOU DO
> SKILLFULLY FOR THE LORD?

Journaling

18

SOMEONE TO
Stick Up
FOR YOU

I was doing poorly in high school chemistry, so Dad went to the school teacher conference. (This memory brings a little bit of throw-up to my throat even now.) He let the teacher have it – right there in front of God and everybody. How come everyone else in the class was doing so well? (He made that teacher show him the grade book.) And why was his daughter doing so poorly?

Rotten, dirty, no-good, scoundrel of a teacher.

It never occurred to him that I was mostly an idiot. Well, not a complete idiot: just where anything happened in the math or science hallway at school.

He seemed to think I was intelligent, so surely the teacher was the problem.

The teacher probably attended four years of therapy afterward, but I kind of like that Dad went to school and stuck up for me.

Listen to this verse that describes how God takes cares of His people: "Happy are you, O Israel! Who is like you, a people saved by the LORD, the shield of your help, and the sword of your triumph! Your enemies shall come fawning to you, and you shall tread upon their backs." (Deuteronomy 33:29) Do you see that verse starts with the word "happy"? You can be happy, knowing the Lord has your back. If you have enemies, you can trust the Lord is going to do something about it. He will take care of your enemies at the proper time, and they will be sorry.

> IS THERE SOMEONE WHO HAS BEEN
> AN ENEMY TO YOU? SOMEONE WHO HAS
> TRIED TO DESTROY YOUR LIFE?
> WRITE TO GOD ABOUT YOUR BELIEF
> THAT HE WILL TAKE CARE OF THIS ENEMY.

19

SOMEONE TO
Teach You
WHAT YOU NEED TO KNOW

The front room table is where all the crying happened. There sat Dad, every math book that came my way, and me.

The front room table is where Dad taught me – when I was in high school – how to make my numbers correctly so that they were easily discernible from one another.

I learned to make eights like a snowman with two circles, because what is this ridiculous figure-eight thing? I learned to make fives and threes with flat tops, sevens with a tag on the left, fours with a left-hand line that curved outward, so as not to be confused with a closed nine, and twos with a nice swoop on the bottom so they could not possibly look like a seven.

The front room table is where I learned *not* to conserve the forests. "We can afford as much paper as you need, so write big," Dad said. By big, he meant like you used to write on your Indian Chief Tablet in first grade. No child of his was ever going to get a math problem wrong because the teacher couldn't read it.

The front room table is where I learned to label each math problem with the problem number from the book and then to circle that number. It would be a shame if the teacher were to think that problem number was actually part of the math problem.

Then, after those lessons were mastered, Dad taught me how to work the actual math equations.

You would have to know how dumb I am in math, to appreciate that Dad spent hours at the front room table with me, helping me with algebra. He was so patient.

He taught me that the words in the problems had to be carried through just like the numbers did. If there are 10 apples and 10 oranges, you always have to write the words *apples* and *oranges* and treat those just like the numbers. I find it slightly amusing now that the ability to apply the word part is the only lesson I was able to carry into adulthood.

As I write this, I'm getting ready to start back to school

as a high school Spanish teacher. I've spent so much time thinking about how to help my students. I've prayed for them. I've worked hard to make the room cozy and a good learning environment. Can you imagine how much more caring and excellent God is as a teacher? Imagine how much He understands what you need as an individual.

Psalm 119:12 says, "Blessed are you, O LORD; teach me your statutes!" God is such a patient teacher. He will work on the details with you. He'll give you all the time in the world. He'll buy you as much paper as you need so that you can do well.

> What do you think God is
> trying to teach you
> in this season of your life?

20

SOMEONE TO

Respond

TO YOUR REQUEST

I must have been in high school when my parents drove my friends and me all the way to Riverton, to the roller skating rink, for my birthday party.

I remember trying to turn smoothly around the corner, by putting my right skate over my left. I'm sure it looked seamless. Those were the days when I dreamed of slow skating with a boy, but it was only a dream. At least I had Lionel Richie singing "Hello." *Yes, it's me you're looking for.*

Taking an intermission from my romantic interlude with my own imagination, I stopped to ask Dad if he would please buy me and my friends snacks from the concession stand.

"No," he said.

"Please, Dad!" I begged.

There was mention of how much this party was already costing, stressed looks between both parents, and then he gave in.

I'm ashamed of the memory now, that I was so thoughtless when I was already receiving so much from my parents. But Dad did give me what I wanted. This story makes me think most about the entitlement wealthy parents bestow on their children. Can you believe my dad allowed me to beg and get my way with him?

Jesus says to his disciples, "If you ask me anything in my name, I will do it" (John 14:14). God entitles you to ask for anything in the name of His Son. He tells you clearly that He likes it when you pray for something over and over again. He does say "No" at times (you wouldn't want to be spoiled *rotten*), but He will reward you when you keep asking and asking and asking for something.

> WHAT DO YOU WANT TO ASK
> THE FATHER FOR TODAY?

Journaling

21

SOMEONE TO GIVE YOU

Eternal

LIFE

When my dad's stepdad passed away from Lou Gehrig's disease, we went to view the body. I remember as a young person being freaked out by the whole thing: seeing a dead body for the first time. I wasn't close to Grandpa, really, so it wasn't distressing emotionally, but a funeral home, coffin, and dead body were disturbing.

Dad stood next to me and talked to me frankly about Grandpa's death. I remember him telling me that all we were looking at was just a body. The soul was gone from it. Then he forced me to do something. He made me reach out my hand and touch Grandpa's dead, cold body.

I recoiled at the thought, but Dad grabbed my fingers and made me lay them on Grandpa's skin. It was awful.

I had no idea that years later I would attend a substantial number of funerals, because of my roles as pianist and then pastor's wife. Understanding death was a valuable lesson.

As I write this, it has now been well over a year since my dad went to be with the Lord. He passed away from a heart attack on a snowmobile. But in the few years before he died, he kept saying, in his matter-of-fact way, that he was getting older and wouldn't be around forever. His words really helped prepare me for his death.

God is a Father who makes you think about death and life. He makes you take a realistic look at your perishing body. But Jesus also tells us this about the Father: "For God so loved the world, that he gave his only Son, that whoever believes in him should not perish but have eternal life" (John 3:16). A good Father never wants to be separated from His children, and God wants you to be with Him forever.

WRITE TO GOD ABOUT YOUR THOUGHTS
ON SPENDING ETERNITY WITH HIM.

Journaling

22

SOMEONE WHO ALWAYS HAS

Time

FOR YOU

"Wanna go with me downtown?" Dad would say.

"Sure!" I would say. It's nice when your dad wants you to be with him.

So I would climb up in the truck, and we would drive the few blocks down to Ace Hardware. He would hop out of the truck a half second after he pulled the key out of the ignition, and before I could get my door open he would be halfway down the sidewalk.

"Hurry up. I ain't waitin' on ya," he would holler over his shoulder.

Dad had short legs, but he could move them at a fast pace. Work boots coming down solid on the sidewalk. Dad was always on a mission, and I could even hear it in the way he breathed. Whatever he was doing at the moment was always urgent and required a swift approach.

We would enter the hardware store, and Dad would quickly find what he needed and head to the checkout. And that is when he slowed down. "Rog!" the store clerk would shout out. Because of course my dad was known by first name at the hardware store. In fact, no matter where we went, people seemed to know Dad and to be happy to see him.

Dad would energetically plop his purchase down on the counter, and proceed to have a friendly, unhurried conversation with the clerk. It seemed that the shopping needed to be done with a finger snap, but the people needed to be enjoyed slowly.

The Apostle Luke tells this story: "And behold, there was a man named Zacchaeus. He was a chief tax collector and was rich. And he was seeking to see who Jesus was, but on account of the crowd he could not, because he was small in stature. So he ran on ahead and climbed up into a sycamore tree to see him, for he was about to pass that way. And when Jesus came to the place, he looked up and said to him, 'Zacchaeus, hurry and come down, for I must stay at your house today.'" (Luke 19:2-5)

Jesus loved people and took time for them, the way my

dad did. You'll find that God the Father is really busy at work, but never too busy to talk to you.

> The Father has time for you right now. What would you like to talk to Him about?

23

SOMEONE TO

Heal

YOUR BROKEN PLACES

D ad fixed things.

He got to a place in life where he could afford to replace broken items, but he always made the repairs instead. His momma grew up during the Depression, and he himself knew poverty in the early years of his life. So, there was no wasting of things if you could get a little more life out of them.

Fix-it guys would call him a machinist, but I say he was an artist. He chose, as his artistic medium, an acetylene torch instead of a paintbrush or sculpting clay.

In our front room there used to be a window that opened into the garage. I imagine it didn't originally open into the garage, but that the garage itself was a construction afterthought. Dad would spend many evenings in the garage repairing things that had motors, and these rotated according to season. Boat motors and motorcycle engines in the summers. Snowmobile engines in the winter.

The phone would ring inside the house. If it were for Dad, I would pull the phone to the front room. The phone, in those days, was attached to a spiral cord and then to a phone base hung on the wall. I would use the hand crank to open the window into the garage.

"Daaaaad!" I would yell, because a certain volume is necessary to be heard over things that require gasoline in order to run. "Phone!"

He would bring over his grease-covered hands to grab the phone. I would hand it out to him and then enjoy the smell of fumes wafting inside the house. It may have smelled bad, but I knew there wasn't anything my dad couldn't fix in that garage.

We read this about Jesus: "And all the crowd sought to touch him, for power came out from him and healed them all" (Luke 6:19). Jesus could fix people: not just physically, but the whole person. So you can know that God is the kind of Father who can fix any problem you bring to Him.

WHAT IS BROKEN THAT NEEDS
THE HEALING TOUCH OF JESUS
IN YOUR LIFE TODAY?

24

SOMEONE TO VALUE THE

Color

OF YOUR SKIN

The washer and dryer were in the kitchen when I was young, and I could smell the oil from Dad's overalls every night, as he pulled them off and handed them to Mom for washing.

Dad was an employee of Amoco Oil Production, where he worked with several Indians from the Shoshoni and Arapahoe tribes. I say "Indians," because that is what we all said when we were growing up, and that's still the going word in my hometown.

There was undeniable prejudice against Indians in those days. There were stereotypes and a distinction between reservation life and town life. I admit that my dad threw out a politically incorrect joke on occasion (before political correctness got us all thinking about our choice of words). But he was just as warm and outgoing toward the Indian people as he was to anyone else. He worked with some good, hardworking Indian men, who earned his respect.

One time my dad did an act of service for an Indian, and the man was so appreciative that he gave Dad a peace pipe. Indian men were not known to give peace pipes to white men as gifts. My dad was so proud and honored by the gift that he hung it above his desk, right next to the pictures of his kids.

In Revelation 7:9, we read, "After this I looked, and behold, a great multitude that no one could number, from every nation, from all tribes and peoples and languages, standing before the throne and before the Lamb, clothed in white robes, with palm branches in their hands." You need to know the Father values where you came from. He values your people, your tribe, your language. You will be welcome at his throne.

> TALK TO THE FATHER ABOUT ANY INJUSTICE
> YOU'VE FELT IN YOUR LIFE
> BECAUSE OF YOUR RACE OR ETHNICITY.

Journaling

25

SOMEONE GOOD TO

Work

FOR

One of the science lessons Dad inadvertently taught me was about surface tension. According to the Merriam-Webster dictionary, surface tension is "the force that causes the molecules on the surface of a liquid to be pushed together and form a layer."

If I didn't fill his milk glass to the top, Dad would throw a fit.

"You call that full?" he would say.

I would look at the glass, and then at him.

He would look back at me expectantly, communicating nonverbally that I had not yet adequately completed my job of pouring.

"It's full," I would say.

"Fill it up," he would say, followed by his determined, we-will-be-here-until-you-get-this-right look.

I would pour a bit more.

"Keep going," he would say.

You know those vanishing-edge swimming pools? You can get the same effect with a glass of milk.

Not long ago my husband poured me a mug full of coffee. "Can you please fill it all the way?" I said.

"Really?" he said, looking at the mug.

That is when I realized I was anxious that all was wrong with the world until surface tension was the only thing holding the liquid in my cup.

Paul gives us this instruction, and it helps us understand something about who God is as Father: "Whatever you do, work heartily, as for the Lord and not for men, knowing that from the Lord you will receive the inheritance as your reward. You are serving the Lord Christ" (Colossians 3:23-24).

God is the kind of Father who has an incredibly high standard for how things get done, and He expects us to do everything heartily, like filling a glass all the way to the brim. But He also is a Father who rewards our exceptional work done in his service.

> WHAT WORK IS IN FRONT OF YOU TODAY,
> AND HOW CAN YOU DO THAT WORK
> ALL THE WAY TO THE BRIM?

Journaling

26

SOMEONE TO EXPRESS

Love

FOR YOU

When we met with the mortician after Dad went to be with the Lord, we took clothes for him to be buried in. The mortician looked at the wool socks with chagrin. "These are the same socks we took off of him," he said, not knowing these were Dad's *good* wool socks. We all burst out laughing, which I imagine is inappropriate when you are around the table to plan your father's funeral.

Every night before going to bed, Dad would pull off his wool socks. "Sock attack!" he would say. Then he would throw his dirty socks in my face.

"Daaaaaad!" I would yell, tossing his nasty socks onto the floor.

It was a tender, father-daughter ritual. Such sweet memories, these.

I have tender, albeit less stinky, memories with God as my Father – ways he demonstrated his affection for me. Like the day we moved all of our possessions into a storage unit, and the moment we placed the last item inside, the sky unleashed a torrent of rain. I stood under the canopy of the storage unit roof and thanked God for helping us get our stuff under cover before he dumped water. As I thanked him, the rain stopped and a brilliant rainbow came into view, right in front of us.

The psalmist sings, "Great is your steadfast love toward me" (Psalm 86:13a). The love of the Father is great, in one way, because it's personal. He sees what we need in the moment, and He shows His love regularly in ways that are specific to our needs. God may not throw socks, but you can expect Him to find unique ways to express His love for you.

> WRITE A PRAYER ASKING GOD TO SHOW HIS LOVE
> TO YOU IN A SPECIAL WAY TODAY.
> YOU CAN ASK FOR THAT, YOU KNOW.

Journaling

27

Someone to

Reward

Your Best Efforts

The deal was $20 for straight A's or $1 for every A. There was no bending in the agreement. If you got all A's except for one class, it was still just $1 each.

I never got $20, but I always tried.

The offer extended to the grandkids. When my daughter walked across the stage wearing her *summa cum laude* cord, I gave Dad part of the credit for motivating her. He would always ask how the grades were coming, and there was a great love and attentiveness in the asking. It is very special to know someone cares about how you're doing.

In Psalm 62:12, we read an encouraging truth: "...to you, O Lord, belongs steadfast love. For you will render to a man according to his work" (Psalm

62:12). The psalmist connects God's love with God's reward. The Father sees your labor and will reward you for work well done. He'll make it worth the effort and sacrifice you put into doing what is right and good.

> WHAT GOOD WORK HAVE YOU BEEN DOING,
>
> FOR WHICH YOU ANTICIPATE A REWARD
>
> FROM THE FATHER?

Journaling

28

B.U.R.P.

It stands for "Blow Up Roger's Place," because my dad's cement driveway was *the* gathering place on the Fourth of July, and the family needed a name for such a grand tradition. The day started with lawn chairs down on Main Street and waiting for the parade colors to pass by, followed by the Lander Valley Junior High School marching band. Later Mom would prep burgers for the grill and make baked beans with brown sugar and bacon, along with potato salad.

In the afternoon, the boys would leave to go to the fireworks stand. They would come back with huge bags of fireworks, the cost of which I imagine would have purchased a new car if saved over the years. Soon, the boys would begin blow up the boring stuff: hundreds of bottle rockets and firecrackers. How can that stay interesting for so many hours in a row?

When it got dark outside, the girls (aunts and cousins and such) would grab jackets and blankets (because it was a cool July evening in Wyoming) and head out to the front porch for the *real* fireworks: the ooooh-ahhhh ones. Dad would produce sparklers for the little kids and big, in-the-sky sparklies for the womenfolk.

When it was all over and we could be diagnosed with black lung, Dad would pull out the broom and clean up the debris. On the driveway and in the street and all the way to the neighbor's front yard would be hundreds of dollars reduced to paper bits, ash, and shrapnel.

Dad was an investor. He invested in the stock market and got a good return. He invested in fireworks and, at least in his way of thinking, got a good return in family celebration.

God is the same kind of Father, who will spend an exorbitant amount of energy just to hear you say, "Ooooh! Ahhhh!" In Psalm 77:14 we read, "You are the God who works wonders; you have made known your might among the peoples."

WRITE ABOUT A TIME WHEN GOD
PERFORMED SOMETHING IN FRONT OF YOU
THAT CAUSED YOU OOOOH AND AHHHH.

Journaling

29

SOMEONE TO

Serve

YOU

L iving in Wyoming meant weeks of snowfall, so Dad bought a four-wheeler ATV. He put a snowplow blade on the front and would plow everything.

Everything.

Including the backyard.

My mom objected to the way he ruined the pristine view from our living room window. Dad insisted it was practical, giving him a dry walkway from the house to the wood pile and shed in the backyard. When it snowed, we would look at it fast, before Dad got home.

Dad also plowed the front driveway and our front side-walk. Then he kept going. He went to the west and cleared the neighbor's sidewalk, and to the east to clear the neighbor's sidewalk.

Dad had an expression he would use when I was self-ish (which I think must have been often, because I sure heard him say it to me a lot.) "Well, you one-way lookin' thing," he would say.

Dad had no selfish bones in him. He always looked in other people's direction, and if he had some way he could help them out, he would do it. He would go as far as his resources would allow. That included always plowing farther than his own sidewalk.

We read in Matthew 20:28 that "the Son of Man came not to be served but to serve, and to give his life as a ransom for many." Jesus has always been looking your way, seeing what you need. It's crazy to think about, but the Father looks to serve you. He's looking for ways to help you out, as far as His resources will allow, and He has limitless resources.

> DESCRIBE HOW IT FEELS TO KNOW THAT
> JESUS CAME TO SERVE YOUR NEEDS.

Journaling

30

SOMEONE TO

Be There

WHEN YOU FAIL

My blood pounded in my ears when Grandma pulled out the keys to her '63 Chevy and told me it would be mine to borrow in high school, as soon as I got my driver's license. It was a massive tank-like vehicle with no power steering, but I didn't care. I was going to have my own car.

The car even came with an ah-ooga horn, which malfunctioned once when I was driving downtown. The sound was so loud and sickly that drivers around me started pulling over because they thought some kind of emergency vehicle was coming.

I loved that car, but I had trouble remembering to put gas in it. When I got around the block from our house one day and ran out of gas, Dad brought me gas and a scowl. When I got down to Taco John's one night and ran out of gas in the dark, Dad brought me gas and a scowl.

He always came to my rescue, and he even spared me verbal lectures. Although he said plenty with his eyebrows, he always came.

In the same way, we discover, "The steadfast love of the LORD never ceases; his mercies never come to an end" (Lamentations 3:22). When we know we've messed up and God should let us have it, instead we find a ridiculous, undeserved mercy from Him.

What does God do when you fail over and over? He keeps coming when you call.

HAVE YOU DONE SOMETHING WRONG?
WRITE TO THE LORD ABOUT IT,
EXPECTING A MERCIFUL RESPONSE
FROM HIS GREAT LOVE FOR YOU.

Journaling

31

If you're going to take an elderly woman home from church and not pay attention at an icy intersection, make sure you are behind your own father's truck. This is exactly what I did. When I realized the light was red and he was stopping, it was too late. Even the brake-pumping he taught me did very little to stop the inevitable.

So this sweet elderly woman and I gritted our teeth, as my old Chevy tapped the back bumper of my dad's truck and slowly pushed it out into the intersection.

I finally got my car stopped. And then I got a pointed-finger lecture through the window of the car. Something about why couldn't I pay attention and needing to slow down sooner on ice and think about what if it hadn't been him I had hit.

Something like that.

When I do something that's displeasing to the Lord, I can feel His finger pointing a lecture at me. Sometimes it's just a feeling that He's looking at me in disappointment, which is the most painful. In Proverbs 3:12, we learn, "For the LORD reproves him whom he loves, as a father the son in whom he delights."

On the day I rear-ended my dad's truck, what I felt most from Dad was the "What if?" What if I had been going faster? What if I had crashed harder? What if I had pushed Dad's truck into another car? What if any of us had gotten hurt? The pointing finger was connected to a fear of how much worse things could have been. And fear for safety comes from the heart of a loving father who wants to protect his kid.

> DESCRIBE A TIME WHEN YOU EXPERIENCED
> GOD POINTING HIS FINGER IN REPROOF,
> BUT YOU KNEW HE WAS TEACHING YOU
> TO THINK ABOUT THE "WHAT IF?"

32

SOMEONE TO HOLD YOU WHEN YOUR
Heart
IS CRUSHED

My dad's little sister came by the house after enduring many grueling hours on jury duty. The jury she was on had found the accused man guilty of murder and sentenced him.

She walked in the door and fell into my dad's arms, sobbing. He held her for the longest time until she calmed down, and then he talked her through the experience. I'll never forget how strong and tender he seemed, all at the same time.

When I got the call that dad had died on his snowmobile, my heart was broken. It still hurts. But immediately, I could feel how near the Lord was to me. He whispered encouragement to me the whole time I traveled home. He strengthened me as we prepared for the funeral. He was a calming presence for months after Dad died and I was awake at night, sobbing into my pillow.

I have found this to be true: "The LORD is near to the brokenhearted and saves the crushed in spirit" (Psalm 34:18). It is beautiful to me that my own dad demonstrated loving arms to me, on the day my aunt came by the house and collapsed into his strong embrace. It feels just like that to know God as Father. So be confident that you can walk into the strong arms of God when you need to fall apart.

IS YOUR HEART CRUSHED TODAY?
TALK TO GOD ABOUT IT. HE IS NEAR.

Journaling

33

Someone to

Say

You'll Be Okay

I was riding my bike so fast, alongside my neighbor, Johnny. "Race ya!" he said.

I don't remember if I was winning, but I do remember when my front wheel hit the end of the pavement and the beginning of the gravel. The handlebars stopped, but I did not. When I landed, it knocked the wind out of me. The next thing I knew I was in Dad's arms, and he was carrying me back to the house.

"You gonna die?" he said.

"Yes," I sobbed, once I could finally breathe again.

Then he laughed – the one where his eyes crinkle in the corners and his head tips back just a little.

"No, you ain't gonna die," he said.

He gently placed me on the couch and patched me up.

We have wrecks in our lives – not on bicycles, but in other ways. Sometimes it's our relationships that crash or our jobs or our health. But Jesus says, "I give them eternal life, and they will never perish, and no one will snatch them out of my hand" (John 10:28). Jesus gives us life, and He makes sure we're secure in His hand.

When your life is a wreck, God will pick you up and patch you up. He will have more hope for you in the moment than you have for yourself.

IF YOU WERE GOING ALONG JUST FINE

AND ALL OF A SUDDEN YOU HIT SOMETHING

THAT TOOK THE WIND OUT OF YOU,

ASK THE LORD TO ENCOURAGE YOU

THAT HE WILL HELP YOU MAKE IT THROUGH.

Journaling

34

SOMEONE TO
Treat the Wounds
YOU'VE CAUSED YOURSELF

Dad was working on replacing the boards in the front deck, and he warned us all a few times not to walk out there, because boards were pulled up.

One afternoon, without thinking, I stepped out the front door and right onto the end of a loose board. Immediately, I fell through the deck, but before I could even react, Dad pulled me out from the hole in the deck and laid me down on the grass.

Blood was dripping from a gash in my leg.

It is amazing that Dad could yell at me about not listening to instructions while extricating me from the deck and gently tending my wound.

So many of our wounds come from our own foolishness. I think about the relationship troubles I've gotten myself into over my decades of life, and how often they could have been avoided if I had just followed God's precepts. I can picture myself lying there bleeding while the Holy Spirit says, "If you had just listened, girl!" But always those words come while he's forgiving me and teaching me and comforting my wounded soul.

Psalm 147:3 says, "He heals the brokenhearted and binds up their wounds." Why doesn't the Father just let us lie there and suffer the consequences of what we've done? Because He loves us so much. His tender mercy is never-ending. God is the kind of Father who gives specific instructions, but He loves us and cares for us even when we fail to keep His instructions.

WRITE ABOUT THE LATEST THING YOU'VE MESSED UP BECAUSE YOU BLATANTLY WENT AGAINST GOD'S INSTRUCTIONS TO YOU. WHAT DO YOU THINK ABOUT THE AMAZING TRUTH THAT GOD FORGIVES OUR DISOBEDIENCE AND WILL EVEN HELP US GET BACK ON OUR FEET?

Journaling

35

SOMEONE TO TEACH YOU

Necessary

SKILLS

Dad tortured me with car knowledge. I remember trying ever so hard to look interested, as he walked me through my first owner's manual. I stifled a yawn behind his back when he showed me where the jack was. I rolled my eyes when he made me actually change a tire.

Spark plugs? Seriously, who cares how to change a spark plug? And did he really expect me to get down on that rolling thingy that takes you under the car, and change the oil?

It was even worse when he took me out in the old Ford pickup to teach me how to drive a stick shift.

Worst. Day. Ever.

I'm pretty sure my chiropractic visits now stem from

those days of jolting stick shift practice.

Years later, Dad would laugh and talk about those lessons, as if they were fun and we were just havin' a good old time. Dads can be so annoying about that kind of stuff.

Okay, so I own a stick shift now.

What of it?

Peter tells the believers to, "Humble yourselves, therefore, under the mighty hand of God so that at the proper time he may exalt you" (1 Peter 5:6). Sometimes God has a heavy hand in teaching us skills we need to know but don't really want to learn – like the skill of forgiving people, which is worse than a week of stick shift practice. God will make you do things you don't want to do. He'll teach you things you have no interest in learning. That's part of the good-Father thing. But after the heavy hand of instruction, there is always the exaltation of your soul.

> WHAT UNPLEASANT LESSON IS GOD TRYING TO TEACH YOU RIGHT NOW?

36

SOMEONE TO GIVE YOU

Good

THINGS

It was just a few days before Christmas, and Dad hollered for me to get into the truck. Downtown we went, to one of the few nice shops in that little town of 7,000. Wyoming Wildwood was a place that smelled good when you walked in. The back was a florist's shop, and the front had glass shelving full of breakable stuff that moms would probably like to get for Christmas.

Dad and I looked at porcelain things and pretty kitchen items. Sniffed some perfumes. Then we stood in front of a case filled with jewelry, and he asked me a question: "If you could ask for one thing for Christmas, what would it be?"

"I think Mom has already bought my gifts," I said.

"I didn't ask you what your mom had bought. I asked what you would want," he said.

Feeling awkward, I looked into the jewelry case and jokingly said, "How about that emerald necklace? I love that. But make sure you get me the matching stud emerald earrings to go with it."

We laughed at my audacity and continued shopping for Mom.

Thirty years later, I still wear that necklace and matching earrings.

Here is one of my favorite passages in the Bible, from Jesus' own lips: "Which one of you, if his son asks him for bread, will give him a stone? Or if he asks for a fish, will give him a serpent? If you then, who are evil, know how to give good gifts to your children, how much more will your Father who is in heaven give good things to those who ask him!" (Matthew 7:9-11)

My dad was an ordinary, sinful man, yet he knew how to shower his girl with love and protection and even unnecessary jewelry. How much more will your Father give to you?

> DESCRIBE A TIME WHEN GOD
> GAVE YOU SOMETHING GOOD.

Journaling

37

It was my first semester in college, and I was heading into finals with my first-ever F because zoology was one step beyond the reach of my brain. It was written and taught in the foreign language of science, and I could not comprehend it.

I was going to school on a full scholarship that demanded a certain GPA. Paralyzed with fear, I wondered what would happen to my scholarship if I were to fail this class. Worse than imagining losing my scholarship was the stomach-knotting worry of what my dad would say when he heard I was failing.

I finally worked up the courage to dial home. I talked to Dad and told him of the coming doom.

"So?" he said calmly, after he heard me out.

Silence.

"So?" I said.

"So? Tell me the worst possible outcome of this situation," he said.

"I could go on academic probation," I said.

"Okay," he said.

"I would have to retake the class. It's a required class."

"Okay."

"I might lose my scholarship."

"Okay."

Dad's calmness slowed my heart rate. His perspective gave me hope that my entire life was not about to be destroyed by zoology.

I found a tutor to help me study for the final, and I passed that class with a C+.

When my daughter started a new job and was feeling frustrated by the mistakes she was making, I had to teach her that failing is a regular part of our lives. Everyone messes up at work sometimes, even the seasoned professionals. We also make wrong moves in relationships at times. Parents have moments of failure. Spouses blow it. Because we are sinful, weak humans, it's important that we know how God is going to respond to our failures.

Peter advocates "casting all your anxieties on him, because he cares for you" (1 Peter 5:7). Is there any greater anxiety than the potential humiliation of blowing it? But we are encouraged to take *all* our anxieties to the Lord. Just like my dad responded to my failures, God is not going to hammer us for failing, because He cares about us. He listens and helps. So when you're failing and filled with anxiety, call God. He's not ruffled by anything you have going on, and He cares about you.

WRITE TO THE LORD ABOUT SOMETHING
IN WHICH YOU FEAR YOU WILL FAIL.

Journaling

38

SOMEONE TO

Show Love

TO YOU

I was in college before I realized my dad had never told me he loved me, at least not that I could remember. I don't know what brought that fact to my attention, but at first I felt hurt. What dad doesn't say, "I love you" to his little girl?

I would talk to him on the phone from my dorm room in Texas, and when we were done I would say, "I love you, Dad."

"Okay, kid," he would say.

And then I realized he had never needed to say it. Everything he did for me spoke love, and that's why I had never noticed the words weren't coming out of his mouth. I knew I was loved, and that was enough.

As I got older, he did start speaking something to me. He would wrap his arms around me and pat my back so hard I would grit my teeth. And he would speak a pronouncement loud enough for everyone to hear: "This is my daughter, in whom I am well pleased."

He would say this over me for no good reason. I mean, it was more like a greeting and statement of fact, rather than a reward for some amazing accomplishment. So I think it was his own way of getting the words "I love you" out of his mouth.

Once my back healed up from the pounding, I felt really good inside.

How does God express His love for us? Paul says, "But God shows his love for us in that while we were still sinners, Christ died for us" (Romans 5:8). You want to know so badly that God loves you, but it's important to know that He is a Father who tends to demonstrate love instead of saying it in words.

He shows you His love every day. Every time you think of the cross, you know it. He gave up everything to get you.

> HOW DOES REMEMBERING CHRIST'S
> SACRIFICE BRING THE LOVE OF GOD
> CLOSE TO YOUR HEART TODAY?

Journaling

39

SOMEONE TO

Watch Over

YOUR LIFE

D ad pushed me to be a nursing major. A practical man, he figured the world always would need a nurse, so I would always have a job if I became one.Of course, he seemed unable to associate my tears over math and science with my inability to get through a nursing program. To say nothing of the fact that I was on the ditzy side of things and could imagine myself saying, "Wait, did I give you that morphine already? I can't remember." I would have killed some patient for sure.

The end of my freshman year of college, I was in an English writing class. My professor, a stately, gentle elderly woman, called me to her desk at the front of the room. In her hand she was holding the paper I had just turned in.

"What is your major?" she asked.

"Nursing," I said.

She told me she was very impressed with my writing, and then she said, "Why are you not an English major?"

"I don't know," I said.

On my walk home from that class, my mind went back to all the success I had experienced in literature, penmanship, and spelling. (I once went to the Wyoming state spelling bee as an alternate, but I try not to let it go to my head.) One of my favorite memories was the daily journal we kept in third grade, and how much I enjoyed it when our teacher read from *Doctor Doolittle* every afternoon after lunch. In high school, I excelled in giving speeches and signed up, on purpose, to take a Shakespeare class. I read books every night until my mother feared I would go blind. "Just one more chapter," I always begged.

By the time I returned to my dorm room, I had decided it was ridiculous to be a nurse, and the thought of an English degree made my heart race.

But how to tell Dad? Respect for him made me dread the conversation, but I called immediately anyway. I don't remember what he said that day, but I also don't remember him arguing against me changing majors. Considering that the man spelled phonetically and did not believe paragraph breaks were a necessary part of written communication, I imagine he was very disappointed with me going the direction of words instead of medicine. Nevertheless, I hold an English degree and Spanish minor from the University of Mary Hardin-Baylor.

Before my dad went to be with the Lord, I gave him a rough draft of this book for Father's Day, and he got tears in his eyes as he read it. So I figure there was no grudge on his part that I changed majors. He just wanted me to be able to put food on the table.

God is the kind of Father who wants to make sure you're taken care of. In Psalm 121:5, we read, "The Lord is your keeper." God watches over your work, your paycheck, and your bills. He cares about the state of your fridge and if you have adequate clothing and shelter. You're not on your own.

> HOW HAVE YOU SEEN GOD
> GUIDING YOU IN YOUR WORK AND
> CARING FOR YOUR NEEDS?

Journaling

40

"So, ummmmmmm, Daaaaaddy?"

"Yes?" he said.

"So, um, I was just wondering. Um. I just wanted to ask, but you don't have to if you don't want to. It's not a big deal..."

"Would ya just tell me what ya want?" he said. He was annoyed to have to pull the request out of me.

"So there's this writer's conference I want to go to in the fall, but I, uh, I can't really afford to go."

Dad skirted around giving me an actual *Yes*, so I kind of took that as a *No*. Later I said something to Mom, and she said, "You do know he intends to pay for you to go to the conference, right?"

And so I went.

When I come to God in prayer, I imagine him getting annoyed if I don't just come out with it and tell him what I need. One of my favorite commands in Scripture is from Jesus in Matthew 7:7. "Ask, and it will be given to you; seek, and you will find; knock, and it will be opened to you."

I can hear our Heavenly Father saying, "So ask already!" Can you?

WRITE A LIST OF ALL THE THINGS
YOU WANT TO ASK OF GOD.

41

SOMEONE TO SHOW YOU

Mercy

BEFORE ANGER

It was a beautiful summer morning when I learned the phrase "unprotected intersection." That is where I drove the like-new Pontiac Grand Am, which my dad had given me earlier in the month, through an intersection and T-boned the man driving through from the right.

The law: if you approach an unprotected intersection, yield to the right. I will never forget this.

The other driver was okay, although he bloodied his head.

My new car was totaled: the car Dad had been washing meticulously with a Q-tip for years. The car with hardly any miles, that looked like it had just come from the factory.

That happened mid-morning, and I spent the entire day sitting in a daze. By eleven o'clock that night my husband said, "Honey, you need to call him."

I felt physically ill at the thought of calling to tell Dad I totaled the car he had just handed over to me. I couldn't imagine what he would say.

Grabbing the phone, I crawled up onto the bed, knees tucked in close, as if they could offer me some sort of protection or comfort. I dialed Dad's number while my stomach rolled over. I told him what had happened and that we were okay. Then I braced myself for his response.

"Well, do you know what this means?" he said.

"No," I said.

"You're gonna be the best driver out there now. This is going to make you more careful."

That was it. And then he searched hard and found us a replacement car.

Dads can be scary, even the good ones. Our first thought is always that they're going to get mad and let us have it. "But you, O Lord, are a God merciful and gracious, slow to anger and abounding in steadfast love and faithfulness" (Psalm 86:15). A good dad is extraordinarily slow to get angry. I know this, because I've seen this mercy and grace in how my husband has treated our kids over the years. In fact, I think when a kid is in bigger trouble, a good dad becomes even more even-tempered and gentle.

God is worthy to be feared, but He carries this amazing mercy with Him that makes Him a Father you can call with the worst of news. It's going to be okay. You can talk to Him about anything.

> Write about what you think
> makes you afraid to talk to God
> when you've blown it.

Journaling

42

SOMEONE TO

Fill

THE FATHER SPOT

Dad retired from Amoco, but he never stopped working. I suppose that's the way it is for retired folks who can't sit still. He made friends with the men down at NAPA auto parts, and that store became the coffee-shop setting for his retirement years. Every morning at nine o'clock he would put on his boots and head down to NAPA, to make coffee for the guys and to give the company dog some Pup-Peroni treats.

One day when Dad took me out for coffee, he told me stories about the goings-on at NAPA. He told me about a couple of young female employees who were living life aimlessly. He helped one girl with her physics homework so she wouldn't give up and drop out of college.

I could picture him sitting on the bar stool while the young women were supposed to be working, giving them advice about how to live their lives. And I doubt they had requested the advice. Dad wasn't one to speak diplomatically about things. He would just come out and say what he was thinking.

Maybe those girls needed a dad to speak some truth into their lives.

Dad also told me people he helped as they came into the store. When they couldn't seem to figure out what was ailing their vehicles, Dad would invite the person home to his shop and would creatively machine some part that had never existed before. Next thing you know, they were happily on their way, with a working car or snowmobile or whatever gas-powered something that was broken.

So Dad told me all these NAPA stories over a cup of too-expensive coffee. "I guess you could call this my ministry," he said.

I had never heard him use the word "ministry" before. Navy/oil field/NAPA guys don't usually talk about their "ministry," but I could tell that Dad had found his sweet spot. He really loved helping people who needed help.

God loves to help people, too. The psalmist sings, "Father of the fatherless and protector of widows is God in his holy habitation" (Psalm 68:5). God knows everybody needs a strong man to be their dad. He wants to be your Father and take care of you.

> DO YOU FEEL FATHERLESS OR ALONE?
> WRITE AN HONEST NOTE TO GOD
> ABOUT THE DEEP NEED OF YOUR HEART.

Journaling

43

SOMEONE TO POUR DOWN
Blessings
ON YOU

Ten percent was the rule.

"Always give God the first ten percent," Dad would say. "Give God the best, and then live on the rest."

Of course, I happen to know that while ten percent was the *official* offering Dad made to the Lord in one month, it was only the first of many percents to follow down the same path.

What about all the kids Dad helped send to camp? And the thousands of dollars he and Mom gave to send missionaries around the world?

What about the way he would fix a guy's snow machine hood and only charge him for the parts?

What about the way he paid off our credit card debt

and replaced the front bumper of my car that I happened to rub off on a cement median one day?

Or the way he paid for my cousin Tim's garage door repair?

And the stuff he bought to fix things around his mom's house and his in-laws' place?

At Dad's funeral, we heard one word from every single person: generous.

"If you've got it, share it," Dad had said. "That's how I was raised."

Evidently, ten percent was just a warm-up.

Dad showed me what generosity looks like, and I have found the same generous nature in the Father. In Malachi 3:10, the Lord says to his people, "Bring the full tithe into the storehouse, that there may be food in my house. And thereby put me to the test, says the LORD of hosts, if I will not open the windows of heaven for you and pour down for you a blessing until there is no more need."

Can you imagine the windows of Heaven opening for you, and God pouring down blessing until all your needs are taken care of? This is what it means to be in relationship with him. We honor Him with our own giving and generous living in His name, and He outdoes himself, to show His pleasure in how we are living.

How have you been generous in
supporting the Father's work
in this world?

44

SOMEONE TO

Cherish

YOU

It was the time of year when Dad would start to ask, "So, how we doin' for your mom?"

"We" meant *me*, because the man lived in a Wyoming town with shopping as scarce as the population.

It started years ago when he would ask me to buy a few Christmas stocking stuffers for Mom. Pretty soon I was filling the whole stocking. Then it was the stocking and a big chunk of the gifts. All with his money.

I got in a habit of shopping all year long, tucking away treasures in the crawl space, month after month. When we visited in the summer, I would take Dad one large Rubbermaid tub full of gifts. Then, closer to Christmas, I would deliver another.

From a craft fair, I would call and say, "So I found something adorable for Mom here. How much is okay to spend?" He would never give me a limit. He would just tell me to buy it.

It made me hyperventilate sometimes.

"Dad. Give me a limit. Come on," I would say.

"If you think she would like it, just buy it," he would say.

I would text him the amount I had spent, and he would put a check in the mail the second I told him how much the damage was.

Eventually, I got so comfortable with this routine that a lot of times I wouldn't even look at the price of an item. No lie. I would just think, *Mom has got to have this*, and I would go buy it and look at the receipt when I got home.

Lots of times, I even bragged to sales people.

"I do all my dad's Christmas shopping for my mom, so I don't really care how much it costs. He pays for all of it." We would laugh at my audacity, but do you know what the sales ladies would do?

Sigh.

Because how sweet was it that the man wouldn't put a spending limit on his wife for Christmas?

I watched how my dad cherished my mom, and I find

it astounding that our relationship with the Father is often described as Bridegroom and Bride. Isaiah 61:10 says, "I will greatly rejoice in the LORD; my soul shall exult in my God, for he has clothed me with the garments of salvation; he has covered me with the robe of righteousness, as a bridegroom decks himself like a priest with a beautiful headdress, and as a bride adorns herself with her jewels." (Isaiah 61:10) God is going to love you in a way that makes you sigh, a girly, wow-that's-romantic kind of sigh.

MAKE A LIST OF THE FINE CLOTHING
WORN BY THE BRIDE AND GROOM AT A WEDDING.
AS YOU DO, IMAGINE GOD LOVINGLY
CLOTHING YOU WITH
SALVATION AND RIGHTEOUSNESS.

45

SOMEONE TO BE

Gentle

WITH YOU

He loved engines and anything with a motor. Survived Vietnam. Worked the oil fields. He was a man who always had grease under his fingernails, a shop full of tools, and a freezer full of meat he had hunted and processed. Dad was a resourceful man who was not afraid to tackle any repair job, but I never once talked to him on the phone that he didn't tell me what the birds were doing.

His chair swiveled by the living room patio door, and when I called from Montana to home in Wyoming he would tell me about the latest snowmobile he was repairing for a friend. Then I could picture his chair turning, as he would pause and whisper, "Oh, there's a robin."

The cement bird bath sat just outside the door, and he

kept it clean and filled with fresh water. He was such a busy, task-oriented man that it seemed odd he could have the interest and patience to watch what a robin was doing.

Now, let me tell you that God is a great King. He is the Almighty Creator of the universe. He could smoosh us like bugs under his feet. But in Psalm 84:3 we get a glimpse of what it's like in his great hall, and it's not what you would think: "Even the sparrow finds a home, and the swallow a nest for herself, where she may lay her young, at your altars, O LORD of hosts, my King and my God." The sparrow feels comfortable building a nest close to this mighty King. Now that's the kind of strength and tenderness you're looking for in a Father: great power combined with a heart that cares about birds.

> SKETCH A PICTURE OF A GRAND THRONE
> AND A LITTLE SPARROW'S NEST CLOSE TO IT.
> DESCRIBE HOW THIS IMAGE AFFECTS HOW
> YOU FEEL ABOUT CALLING GOD "FATHER."

Journaling

46

SOMEONE TO TAKE YOU
Off-Trail

This will be easy to explain to those of you who grew up playing in powder, but I'm not sure how to describe what I mean to my Texas friends. I know all life comes to a halt for you southern folks when you get a skiff of snow. (Skiff: a layer of snow so thin that blades of grass still show through.)

My dad snowmobiled every winter, in places in Wyoming where they had to put extensions on the reflectors on the side of the road, so you could still see them above eight to ten feet of snow.

Dad wasn't one to follow safe, groomed trails. He looked for meadows full of fresh powder and steep mountainsides yet untouched by snowmobile tracks. When you put a heavy snow machine on top of all that fresh powder, it tends to sink, and dad was always working to defy gravity and stay on top of the snow.

"Just when you think you're gonna get stuck, that's when you gun it," he would say. "Keep your thumb on the throttle." (He who hesitates gets stuck and has to dig out.) To go play in the snow with Dad was to throttle every second on the edge of impossible.

God isn't one for groomed trails, either. To follow him feels like snowmobiling with my dad in the rugged back country of untouched powder and breathtaking vistas. It always feels a little dangerous and a little thrilling at the same time.

Jesus says, "Enter by the narrow gate. For the gate is wide and the way is easy that leads to destruction, and those who enter by it are many. For the gate is narrow and the way is hard that leads to life, and those who find it are few. (Matthew 7:13-14) I think Jesus means: "Broad and flat is the groomed snowmobile trail, and any city slicker could rent a machine and ride on that, but if you want God to be your Father, you're going to have to be willing to ride off trail into the wild where few people are willing to go." This is what it takes to really live.

IN WHAT WAYS HAS FOLLOWING GOD

FORCED YOU TO KEEP YOUR THUMB

TO THE THROTTLE AND HAVE A LITTLE BIT

OF DAREDEVIL IN YOU?

Journaling

47

SOMEONE TO SEE

Worth

IN YOU

It was probably best seen in the boat motor Dad kept alive for 50 years. Every trip to the lake meant a fishing excursion, and a boat motor repair. The repair happened on the lake, with Dad's Leatherman and some electrical tape. He would fix it, and then across the lake we would go. The motor weighed a ton and was nothing pretty to look at, but it was a testimony to Dad's skill with machinery.

Or there was the Christmas day when my folks gave my son the video camera he had been begging for, which he promptly dropped on the floor and broke. Caleb picked it up, his eyes filling with tears. Everyone in the room stopped breathing, and all eyes went to Dad.

You can fix it? we silently asked.

I don't know. That's pretty bad, he silently replied.

We said, *But you can fix it, can't you?*

Out came the tools, and Mom's kitchen bar became Dad's work station. We walked a wide berth around Dad, as he slowly took apart this brand new camera, tiny parts everywhere. His face was grave, as if he were a doctor trying to decide when to call time of death. But then, "Caleb," he said, "here ya go." Repaired.

"Thanks, Grandpa," he said.

We knew. We knew Dad could make it work.

I grew up with this man who fixed things everyone else would take to the dump. He had often watched his own mother pull things out of the dumpster, wash and repair them, and sell them for a decent amount of cash in a garage sale. He learned to live the same way.

In 2 Corinthians 4:16, Paul says, "So we do not lose heart. Though our outer self is wasting away, our inner self is being renewed day by day." I think about my broken-down inner self and have confidence that my Father can fix it – maybe with more than a Leatherman and electrical tape. He is washing me off, fixing me up, and making my soul run like new.

No matter how broken or run down you feel, trust me

that God can repair the most hopeless of souls. He is a Father who pulls you out of the dumpster. He does not throw you in. You just have to know He is really, really good at making things work like new.

> TRY WRITING THIS QUESTION:
> "FATHER, CAN YOU DO SOMETHING
> WITH MY BROKEN PLACES?"

Journaling

48

Someone to

Fill

Your Cupboard

I'm a Wyoming girl, so autumn meant Dad was loading ammunition, sighting in guns, and talking over Opening Day. Then there was the kill, which meant an elk hanging upside down in the garage, its tongue hanging down and creating a bloody icicle attached to the cement floor. It meant the smell of fresh game in the kitchen, Dad deboning meat and Mom wrapping pound after pound of steaks and ground meat into white butcher paper. I would write "elk burger 19-whatever-year" on the package, and this went into the freezer, to supply us with another year of meat to eat.

When I grew up and got married, a generous supply of that meat started coming to our house. "Tell me what you want," Dad would say over the phone. "Roasts? Steaks? Ground beef?" When the VA provided Dad with hearing aids that were powered by Bluetooth technology, he could call and chat with me, hands free, while he sliced meat in the cold garage. I kept him company over the phone, and it seemed a small fee for the hundreds of dollars of meat we'd been given over the years.

Then there was the year we moved into our newly built house, and Mom and Dad drove the 12 hours to come and visit. Pulling weary legs out of the truck, Dad hugged me and said, "I've got your meat."

"Oh great," I said.

"Where ya gonna put all that?" he said.

"Ummm," I replied.

"Matt, get in the truck," Dad said. My husband hopped in, and within an hour they were back from Vann's appliance store and unloading a brand new upright freezer into our garage. Dad was all business in his tone of voice, but his eyes told me he had been delighting in the surprise of buying us a freezer. For twelve hours he had been imagining the look on our faces when he would up and go to the appliance store, like no big deal, and fork over a wad of cash for meat storage. I was used to this sort of thing, of course. Dad loved to plot a ridiculously generous surprise.

Jesus teaches his disciples to pray, "Give us this day our daily bread" (Matthew 6:11). It's a simple phrase, but I've experienced a Father who not only wants to provide but who loves to surprise us with the how. Like the time when Matt and I had two weeks left before a payday and only $11.00 to our names. We were in serious trouble, and I was praying in panic. Then came the mail and a $500 check from an elderly woman back in my home church. She lived on a fixed income. Never had she given us money before, and never did she give us money again. But it was our daily bread, just in the nick of time, and I think the Father enjoyed delivering that little surprise.

> FROM A HEART THAT LOVES AND CARES
> ABOUT YOU, THE FATHER WANTS TO
> GIVE YOU THE FOOD YOU NEED EVERY DAY.
> WRITE DOWN WHAT YOU'VE EATEN
> OVER THE LAST FEW DAYS,
> AND THANK THE FATHER FOR
> GIVING IT TO YOU.

Journaling

49

SOMEONE TO BE YOUR
Rich
DADDY

He wasn't an arrogant man, but there was this one thing he bragged about. We would place our coffee order at Mr. D's grocery store. With the sound of milk steaming in the background, Dad would pull his wallet out of his back pocket. Opening it up, he would lean in close to me and make a show of thumbing through the cash.

"I don't got no money," he would say, as hundreds slid, one after the other, past his thumb. Then always the same conspiratorial smile.

In that simple demonstration, which happened many times in my days as his daughter, Dad would say with his eyes, *See how I've got the cash to take care of you?*

As an adult, those hundreds often got folded up nice

and neat, and got tucked inside my pocket before I would head back to college or back home to Montana.

"There's more where those came from," Dad would say.

A few months after he went to be with the Lord, I was visiting Mom. She brought out Dad's wallet and emptied the hundreds onto the counter. It pained us both deeply.

"Here," she said. "A last gift from your dad." Makes me weep buckets, just thinking about it. I felt bereft, as if every supply of good had been stopped, and the life of being cared for was over. It was just over.

Until the Spirit of God leaned close and whispered in my ear. "It's always been me," He said.

"What?"

"It's always been me. All those hundreds of dollars. The elk meat. The kind, warm hands. The love and surprises. All of that came through me, and your dad was just a conduit." (I say "conduit" in honor of Dad, who loved to talk about electricity and how it flowed like water from one place to another.)

And oh, dear reader, how I wish you were in my kitchen with me right now, as I drip tears all over this laptop of mine. Just one thing, please, for you to take from these humble stories of mine? Will you please accept as truth that all the good you've ever wanted is waiting in the Father's hands for you, and He has entitled you to ask for it?

James tells the believers, "Every good gift and every perfect gift is from above, coming down from the Father of lights with whom there is no variation or shadow due to change" (James 1:17). Everything you need for your life comes from your Father in Heaven.

> SO IF YOU BELIEVE GOD HAS ALL
> THE RESOURCES YOU NEED FOR THIS DAY,
> WHAT DO YOU WANT TO ASK OF HIM?

Journaling

50

SOMEONE TO

Thank

I got a box in the mail from Mom. I cannot count how many boxes Mom has sent me over the years. This one was filled with candy for the family, *Zits* cartoon strips cut out of the newspaper for my teenage boy, a few magazines, and a new shirt for me.

Tucked inside the shirt was a five-dollar bill.

Over the years, five dollars had become a fatherly love note to me that required no explanation. Everything else in the box was from Mom, but it went without saying that the money was from Dad.

"Thanks for the five dollars, Dad," I said over the phone.

"You liked that, did ya?" he said.

That was the extent of the conversation. Me with money in hand. Dad satisfied with a simple word of appreciation.

It seems right to me that one call to action rises throughout the Bible – one thing the Father wants more than anything else: a "thank you." My dad never wanted anything more from me than acknowledgment that he had been good, merciful, and generous to me.

The psalmist sings, "Praise the LORD! Oh give thanks to the LORD, for he is good, for his steadfast love endures forever!" (Psalm 106:1) God is the kind of Father who is going to be good to you even when you haven't asked him to be. Expect it.

> NOW SPEND SOME TIME SAYING THANKS
> FOR EVERY GOOD THING GOD HAS
> BROUGHT YOUR WAY LATELY.

Journaling

51

SOMEONE TO GIVE YOU A REASON TO

Lift

YOUR HEAD

Sometime in the middle of a summer night, Dad gently shook my shoulder. "Wake up," he said. "I want you to see something."

Rubbing my eyes, I followed him, Mom, and my brother out of the house and onto the lawn. "What are we doing?" I asked.

"Look up," he replied.

In the absence of big-city lights, I looked up to see a black sky, over which danced waves of Northern Lights in brilliant and constantly changing arcs of pinks, yellows, blues, and greens. I had never seen this magnificent light show before, and I laughed out loud with enjoyment.

Dad was as delighted to bring the whole family outside

for this experience as if he had planned the fun himself. Of course, he told us that the movement in the sky had a scientific name, the Aurora Borealis. He also gave an accompanying physics lesson in protons and electrons. Solar winds send charged particles into the upper atmosphere, I learned, and when those particles lose energy, their protons produce optical emissions. So we had school and saw a show, all at the same time.

The lights were a fascinating, ever-changing beauty. They were made even more memorable because my dad cared enough to wake us up to enjoy them with him.

King David sings, "The heavens declare the glory of God, and the sky above proclaims his handiwork. Day to day pours out speech, and night to night reveals knowledge" (Psalm 19:1-2). The stars, the moon, and the Northern Lights tell us the message of God's love and greatness. We don't need a science lesson. We just look up, and we feel it.

God comes as our Father, and awakens us in the night. "Look up!" He says.

Describe a time when you looked up

into the sky and saw something

magnificent – maybe even a fierce storm

or a rainbow or a sunset.

How did this experience help you

feel the greatness and yet

the closeness of God?

52

SOMEONE TO

Celebrate

THAT YOU'RE ALIVE

Rising before dark, we would don long johns and then jeans. We would bundle up in winter coats, hats, scarves, and mittens, and slip our feet into snow boots. Then Mom, my brother and I would climb into the car and drive up into Sinks Canyon State Park, which is about fifteen minutes from town. It's called Sinks Canyon because a rushing mountain river sinks into an underground cave and bubbles back to the surface farther down the road. In the summer, it was a great place to feed the fish, but on Easter Sunday it was a sacred place.

Dad would be there ahead of all of us, staking out a camping space (not in high demand when it was twenty-three degrees outside). He had loaded up on breakfast supplies and firewood the day before. On Easter morning, he would set up his camp stove and get a good breakfast going, with bacon sizzling in a skillet and a pile of pancakes coming off the griddle. Meanwhile, water would be heating for hot chocolate.

One by one, the church folks would show up, looking like they'd rolled straight out of bed, but not caring because we were all dressed in the same cowboy-country Wyoming Easter finery. Dad would be high energy, the morning person that he was, heaping plates full of food and laughing. He would have everybody smiling with his charismatic cheerfulness. On Easter mornings, I think he showed himself to be the finest Southern Baptist deacon ever ordained. Certainly he was the happiest.

After breakfast, we would gather around the campfire and sing a worship song about Jesus being risen from the dead, as the sun rose and poked its head into the valley, just before frostbite set in. This was how my dad taught me that Jesus' resurrection is worth celebrating. Not so much with words, but by the trouble he went to early every freezing Easter morning, Dad was declaring his belief that Jesus is alive.

My dad has since passed away, but I am absolutely positive that he and Jesus are now enjoying a campfire and hot chocolate, to celebrate being alive.

Here is the truth: "In Christ shall all be made alive" (1 Corinthians 15:22). This promise is for you, if you will follow Christ. Your Father has made a way for you to have eternal life, and I think it includes a hearty breakfast in the warming sun.

> WHAT DO *YOU* THINK LIFE WILL BE LIKE
> WHEN YOU FINALLY GET TO BE WITH
> THE FATHER WHO CARES
> ABOUT YOU SO MUCH?

Journaling

Afterword

Dad's hands. That's what I noticed when I read these little stories all at once for a final edit.

Dad's hands were wounded and scarred.

They were calloused because he was always working.

His hands woke me up in the morning and threw socks at me at night. They warmed my feet in a storm. They warmed my hands when I was nervous.

Dad's hands cradled a bunny and filled the bird bath every day and wrote joy over my birth.

Dad's hands lifted me up when I crashed. They poured gasoline in my tank when I was careless. They fixed and mended and bandaged.

Dad's hands patted my back in love and pride. They wrote checks when I was broke and sometimes just for fun. They clapped when I played the piano.

God has hands like these. They're not pretty, but they have everything you need. They're strong when you need strong and tender when you need tender. They're generous and good and kind.

The loving hands of God are open to you, and He invites you to call Him Father.

Notes

Epigraph:

Sara Hagerty, "How to Love a Man," June 15, 2015, http://everybitterthingissweet.com/2015/06/how-to-love-a-man/.

Introduction:

Malcolm Gladwell, *Outliers: The Story of Success* (New York: Little, Brown and Company, 2008), 110.

Chapter 1: Someone to Rejoice over You:

Eleanor Smith, *Songs for Little Children, Part 1: A Collection of Songs and Games for Kindergartens and Primary Schools* (Springfield, MA: Milton Bradley Co., 1887), 9.

About the *Author*

Christy Fitzwater is a simple Wyoming girl who, in middle school, asked God if someday she might please write Bible studies for people. She attended the University of Mary Hardin-Baylor, in central Texas, where she met a tall Montana man and agreed to move north with him permanently. Using her English degree and love for Bible truth, she began writing children's Bible lessons for the kids at church and then small group Bible study guides for teenagers and adults. From there she began blogging, at her daughter's suggestion, and she has found great joy in writing short devotionals online. Her goal is to help people get to a place where they can brag that they know God and to live the big, meaningful life God has planned for them. These days Christy considers it romantic to run alongside her husband–doing God's Kingdom work in Big Sky Country, as he preaches good news and she writes about it. Find Christy's devotional writing and Bible-teaching newsletters at christyfitzwater.com.

Also by
CHRISTY FITZWATER

BLAMELESS

Living a Life
Free from Guilt
and Shame

CHRISTY FITZWATER
Foreword by Lisa Jacobson
of Club31Women.com

Don't you get tired of going to bed at night feeling like a failure and then waking up the next day confident that you're going to keep being a failure at just about everything? Add to that the feeling that God is waiting to smoosh you if you mess up or at least to shake his head at you in disappointment.

But it has always been God's plan for you to become blameless.

He's not waiting to hammer you if you blow it. Instead He is daily, patiently shaping you to be faultless.

It may feel too good to be true.

But what if you could believe that God is doing a great work to make you perfect, and what if you could even mark on the door frame how much taller your soul is growing every day? Wouldn't that hope change everything?

"I've read hundreds of books in my life, many of them very good. But few have made me laugh so much, given me so much hope, and made me so eager to share its pages with my friends." ~ Elisabeth Adams

Now available in both digital form and paperback from Loyal Arts Media.

LOYAL
ARTS MEDIA
loyalartsmedia.com

Made in the USA
Lexington, KY
15 June 2018